"Lewis is a poet deft with sonics and image but more than that, casts stories of such particularity and startling turns that each of them begs seconds. If one could ease inside another life for a time and feel the land underfoot, the menace and solace of the natural world, and the throbbing of memory as if it were their own, they would be reading this collection."

-Christine Hope Davis, *Skin, Bone, Feather* (winner of the *Tusculum Review* Poetry Prize)

"These poems lead the reader down seemingly familiar paths (nature, memory, country scenes) only to present unexpected twists – including poems on Kansas twisters – that surprise and delight. Kansas skies yield "puffed clouds innocuous as the beard of God," a full moon becomes a "communion wafer/dissolving in/October dawn," and the town's brush pile is a "smoldering Gehenna." This sophisticated collection shines with story, speculation, history, and humor."

-Maril Crabtree, *Fireflies in the Gathering Dark* (2018 Kansas Notable Book)

"*This Swirling Largesse* is a poetic memoir, an historic, dual journey of a woman's life whose roots trace back to a great-great Choctaw grandmother and the Trail of Tears. Whether we're at the Oklahoma farm reuniting with a father returning from war, birthing a calf, hoeing a black snake to death for eating chicken eggs, riding the trail of transplantation from Alabama to new Indian Territory, or coping with the silence of a country in lockdown during Covid, Lewis always puts us right there with imagery and detail as precise and right on as it gets. With skillful crafting, Lewis turns what could have been an historic account into a poetic triumph. Read *This Swirling Largesse* and enjoy this tour de force."

-Maryfrances Wagner – 6th Missouri Poet Laureate, *Solving for X*

"In *This Swirling Largesse,* Linda Lewis soulfully takes the reader to scenes of rural life that are both tragic and elegant. In *Poteau Twilight,* "A nicker from the filly's stall and the lowing of cattle at intervals measure the bars of twilight." We also read about the desires of Mennonite women and the agony of being sideswiped by a car. The poems in this collection leave the reader wanting more of the skilled and tempered voice of Linda Lewis. Praise for her wonderous observations of common and extraordinary events."

-Gary Lechliter, Managing Editor, *I-70 Review.*

This Swirling Largesse

Poems by Linda M. Lewis

Spartan Press

Spartan Press
Kansas City, Missouri
spartanpress.com

Spartan
Press

Copyright © Linda M. Lewis, 2022
First Edition: 1 3 5 7 9 10 8 6 4 2
ISBN: 978-1-958182-13-0
LCCN: 202294091

Cover photo; Jim Richardson
Author photo: Taton Tubbs

Acknowledgments

As always, thanks to my family, those departed and those still beside me. Special thanks to my cousin James Battles, the family genealogist, who discovered our Choctaw ancestor whom I feature in "River Road." Also to Dora M. Wickson, translation specialist for the Choctaw Nation, for her generous advice about Choctaw vocabulary. Thanks to fellow writers Kristin, Lori, Aubrey, Greg, and Majkin, who accompanied me on this writing journey. Finally, much gratitude to Spartan Press, especially editor/designer Jason Ryberg, for once again taking a chance with me.

"Tornado Alert," "April's in Town Again," and "Sideswipe" were previously published in *I-70 Review*; "Desire" and "Firehouse" in *Thorny Locust*; "Surfeit" and "Spring with Coronavirus" in *Heartland*; and "Encounter" in *Plainsongs*. My sincere appreciation goes to those journals.

In several poems I quote or paraphrase literary texts. Recognition to William Shakespeare for *A Midsummer Night's Dream* ("October Blue Moon") and *Macbeth* ("Nostalgia"), to Andrew Marvell for "To His Coy Mistress" ("Played to a Draw"), to T. S. Eliot for "The Hollow Men" ("Spring with Coronavirus"), and to John Milton for *Paradise Lost* (source for the Adam and Eve whom I follow out of Eden in "Manmaker Comes no More at Twilight" and "Empress of Fair Eden, Snake Called Me").

TABLE OF CONTENTS

Ever a Country Child (I)

River Road (II)

Wither Sooner than Desire (III)

This Swirling Largesse (IV)

To Frank: A Proposal

Will you walk with me, hand-in-hand, my love,
          to this poem's destination?
We'll find forsythia yellow as egg yolk, evergreens
          wearing lace ruanas of knitted snow.
We'll play voyeur as a cardinal twosome return
          to build their twig-and-feather dwelling;
Breathe the scent of catalpa blooms that litter our
          lawn like God's explosion of popcorn;
Perhaps restore a decrepit house, grow tomatoes,
          learn to love sushi and foreign film.
We also must bury stillborn dreams, lodge parents
          side by side in country cemeteries.
But we'll make babies, rose-cheeked and tubby, with
          delectable elbow dimples and double chins.

I.

Ever a Country Child

Now as I was young and easy under the apple boughs . . .

-Dylan Thomas, "Fern Hill"

Washed Away

Floods from spring rain prevent our
navigating the red-dirt county road
to Nixon Cemetery. Rivulets flow across
roadway; torrents of runoff plunge into
ditches too shallow for the overflow.
The road's hills are whittled to bedrock,
as the graded-earth highway melts into
umber mud. My sister and I cannot place
memorial wreaths on matching graves,
cannot pause beneath the aged cedar
that sprinkles fragrance on those alumni
of a marriage bed—positioned as in life
together and asunder. Our visits have
become rare since their departure
(Mama in a nursing home drowning
in the Lethe dementia; our angry father
thrashing, flailing, hauled protesting
away by Death's undertow). I fathom
they are lost—floating, drifting far from
my shore. Buoyed only by memory, they
fade from bone, flesh, sinew into myth.

Resistance

At dusk a tall stranger in pressed khaki opened
our screen door and stepped inside, just as

if he had a claim to the little white rent house
where we lived. All nonchalance, he dropped

a duffle bag on the floor and seated himself
on the edge of Mama's bed. I don't remember

if they embraced or kissed—my long-separated
parents. I do remember that for days past Mama

had made X's on a page of the thin picture book
that hung above the kitchen stove. (I didn't know

the word calendar, didn't comprehend that drawing
X could make time hurry.) I did know the word

father, but this long-legged stranger with buzz cut
and bulky hands did not much resemble one.

He occupied excessive space, seemed to unsettle
the molecules of twilight that hovered round him

in encroaching darkness. He smelled funny too,
a scent that I later came to identify as Camels.

The imposter lifted my little sister onto his lap
and crooned the word "Daddy" as he poked

the shirtfront of his GI uniform. Then he
alternately tapped himself and the photograph

of a somber soldier that Mama kept on her dresser.
I wanted but feared to approach, sensing those

angular limbs would never constitute a refuge
cozy and cushiony like Mama's lap. The open maw

of the duffel yielded treasure—for Mama a flock
of silk scarves, for Baby Sue and me miniature

kimonos in pastel. But my little sister too proved
agnostic: each time the stranger identified

himself as "Daddy," she responded in baby lisp,
"My Daddy in Yokohama."

Juncture

Alongside my father in spring, I slogged
through mud and manure boot-top deep
to pull the calf. Seeking a fulcrum in the mire,
we shifted weight, locked double-hand grips
around skinny blacksnake forelegs—likely
to slither through our grasp. We tugged with
the heifer's contractions until she expelled
her curly-haired baby, addled by
juncture of birth.

Years later early-blooming redwoods—
a scatter of purple commas—sprinkle
a misty page of Oklahoma spring as I drive
south for my father's funeral. During
winter's demise he consigned his body
to be turned and tended by professional
hands—clinical, detached, incapable to
wrest the sentient from thresholds
slippery as death.

Daddy, I wish I could sleeve up, reach into
that vast unseen, grip and tug your hand,
rebirth you into this breathing, moiling world.
Where crops fail or flourish in plenitude,
your labor callouses palms and toughens
the backbone. Where in spring earth yawns,
stretches, blossoms. Where barnyards thaw
to pungent mush and newborn life erupts
at calving time.

Working Hands

Never attentive to her square, sturdy hands, Mama
didn't lotion or pamper them, shape or lacquer her nails.
I thought those hands homely but magic, so adept
they were at making playhouse furniture from packing
crates, quilts from fabric scraps, curls of my limp hair.

On the playground a flying swing peeled back my scalp
like the top off a sardine can. Sewn up, gauze-swathed,
released from hospital into parental hands, I submitted
to mother fingers probing, bandaging and shampooing.
Mama covered the gash with a kerchief handmade
from a silk scarf my father brought her from Japan.

At the Wrangler blue jean factory where she worked,
a monster-ugly sewing machine gobbled Mama's hand,
chewed through a finger, spat her blood. Still her mangled
right hand fluted piecrust, squeezed cow teats, curled
around pliers, ladled jewel-red jelly into canning jars.

Silver

My father was durable, rugged
like the lumber, concrete and
sheetrock of his trade. Taciturn
and hard-edged, he lived by
skilled labor and hard work.
Laid down hard rules and
brooked neither sass nor lip
(skills I studiously crafted).

My father presses eight new
silver dollars into my adult
palm when—years later—I visit
his worksite. Mama surmises
that his largesse declares
parental love for which he has
no language. I take her word
and spend the cold, hard silver.

Picking Season

In Oklahoma's cotton belt,
arthritic granddads to kids
no taller than a cotton stalk
bent and crept, pulling bolls
sunrise to dusk until fields
were picked clean. Schools
shut down in September
as entire families followed
the harvest that crawled
west toward Arizona slower
than larvae of a boll weevil.

In gloved hands, you cradle
cotton bolls scorched brittle
by sun, overflowing with
puff and seed. Flick the wrist
to snap boll from stalk.
Swivel right to left and back
again as you glean parallel
rows, grabbing with both
hands. Jam boll and cotton,
leaves and all into the
heavy sack you drag.

As you fall asleep, count
engorged bolls that waltz
and tango, bob and weave
across your bedroom wall.

Runaways

[Choctaw girls] who had lost one or both parents were placed in [Wheelock Academy], where [they] might remain until they were sixteen.

— Angie Debo, *The Rise and Fall of the Choctaw Republic*

My Grandma Maggie in her early teens lived
at Wheelock, deep in southern Oklahoma,
where orphaned Choctaw girls were dosed on
teaspoons of book knowledge, gallons of cooking,
sewing & laundry prescribed for girls of every tribe.

While schoolmates slept, Maggie & her homesick
older sister crept out of Pushmataha Hall, boarded
a train to their once-was-home. There they were
assigned household jobs for aught that ailed them—
bitterest pill that ever they were forced to swallow.

In the Arena

In a glossy black & white photo, a grinning girl
of eight or nine, wearing a plaid coat and
wind-scrambled hair, grasps the halter of
a Hereford steer who has turned toward

the camera, achieving optimum angle of head
and muzzle—a contrast of white face, dewlap,
underbelly to the dark pelt of shoulder
and forearm, his neck to loin to rump

a monumental silhouette against the brick wall
of the Dodge dealership where the livestock show
was staged. As Registered Herefords are named
to honor the origin of the breed, my calf wore

the moniker Bonnie Prince Charlie. He flourished
from gourmet feeding, frequent currying, scratching
about the ears and a daily ramble guided by a leash
held in a child's hand. Eight hundred pounds of

mighty oak under control of a sixty-five-pound sapling.
My father broke the feisty calf to submit to the halter
by which I guided my oversized pet to the pond for water
then back to the barn for slumber on fragrant hay.

Ever a country child, I knew the source of hamburgers
and pot roast, heard that bulls were for breeding,
steers for eating. None of these facts of livestock
management had to do with Bonnie and me.

As I led my steer round and round the
sales arena, packing house reps rudely yelled
out bids. Buyers dickered for beef on the hoof;
the seller learned outrage and betrayal.

Lost on the Midway

Like a hen leading chicks, the adult in charge paraded
a gaggle of young girls past cotton candy stands,
corndog-on-a-stick, ring toss games, tilt-a-whirl and
the churning Ferris wheel at the Oklahoma State Fair.
Jangling music and a cacophony of smells—hamburgers,
syrup flavors and buttered popcorn—saturated the night.
I suppose the girls slurped in a cheerful row: sno-cone
juice in grape purple and cherry red staining little fingers
and etching colored ribbons down little arms.

I was not among them. Short-changed by the sno-cone
man and left behind by mother hen, I gazed first with
hope, then through tears into the faces of strangers
levitating above me. For some children, the world
assumes the guise of carnival with sugary treats and
merry-go-round music. For others, a cornucopia of
distorting funhouses, hawkers who promise glimpses
of perversity and trips to forbidden paradise.
And carny men who steal from children.

Intruder

Sent by Mama in dwindling daylight to gather
eggs, I froze mid-reach when I encountered
the unblinking claimant's cool-eyed stare.

A reptile squatter—five feet of muscle, grace
and chutzpah—lay ensconced in a nest of the
henhouse, coiled upon itself like a garden hose.

Trespassing among White Leghorns and
Rhode Island Reds, the snake scored in
the sweepstakes of eggs fresh and plentiful.

No more chasing prey, raiding nests of
newborn rodents: sustenance now provided
by the farmer—taste friendly, effort free.

Hens and pullets squawked and scattered as
the marauder browsed the poultry house. For this
fracas, compulsory sentence: the snake must die.

With a gardening hoe, Father severed the fellow's
head. Its body thrashed, whipped, twitched,
writhed. Finally lay still on the henhouse floor.

When settlers with hoe and plow broke the prairie,
they too laid claim to fruits of the land. Now I
gather who first meddled with nature's plan.

Mowing the Iris

A pair of rose bushes and patch of purple and lavender iris constituted the only adornments on the acreage my family rented. Early-blooming and prolific, the iris often flaunted their vibrant frocks before grass and weeds grew tall enough to warrant mowing. In those springs Mama requested that our father spare the iris. But his rusting push mower in swath after swath chewed down and spat out shreds of green jacket and ruffled purple petticoat. So much for the iris ensemble.

Father took note of blossoms on peach trees and heirloom tomatoes. But what of loveliness that exists without promise of edible harvest? Did expedience demand that he sell Fatima, the spirited chestnut filly he rarely rode and never worked on the farm? Did he pause from work to admire sunrise painting our lake in pastels, promiscuous snowflakes dancing down from heaven? What did he make of the abundance of Mama's unruly curls, the cornflower blue of her eyes?

Lord and Lady

Strobes of summer sunlight glinted off glass and metal as
the landlord's king-sized Oldsmobile dipped and swayed
up the one-way lane from the dirt road to our place, stirring
diaphanous clouds of dust. Unannounced, he would show up
to collect his rent; check fences, gates and outbuildings;
dip a hook into his pond to snare bass or crappie
that happened to be biting.

As the landlord removed gear, bait and tackle from the Olds,
his wife—coiffed and svelte and wafting bottled fragrance—
indulged in an unannounced visit with Mama. Mrs. Landlady
disported fashion unlike anything we'd seen or imagined.
Frilly dresses and pencil-skirted suits worn with spike-heel
pumps of snakeskin, shining patent or silk shantung. She
perched on the proffered chair like a goddess enthroned.
Rings adorned her hands, tapered nails painted crayon red.
A slender Chesterfield dangling between her fingers emitted
bluesmoke vines that snaked, swirled and twisted before
fading into the sultry afternoon.

Summoned to wait upon this royalty, Mama—in faded print
housedress and run-down loafers—served up draughts
of iced tea with slices of silence.

Ending in a Draw

Upon turning sixty, Granny cut her waist-length hair
and moved to town. Country life proved lonely when
the kids left—gone to war, migrated to cityscapes,
renting land to start ranches of their own. Granny
didn't drive but in town could walk if need be to church,
the hairdresser or Pasquale's Grocery. She would find
neighbors who cultivated flowers, admired hand
embroidery and crochet, paused for morning coffee
flavored with conversation and store-bought cream.

Unwilling to leave the land, unready to sell cattle,
foxhounds and palomino mare, Grandpa Jim refused
to budge. He considered himself a cowman, not
a city dude. He could fry eggs and brew coffee, he
figured, and deliver his laundry for Granny to wash.
To the consternation of family, they lived apart; she
in town, he out on the ranch. But Time's wingèd chariot
overtook palomino and rider. Pa Jim now lies beside
Granny in the town cemetery, not the country one.

Country Justice

We heard about the shooting from Uncle Homer:
"She got him right through the shoulder after he
came home on Saturday night, or rather early

Sunday morning, drunker than a skunk." Here
our parents sent us from the room, and we
heard no more. But we jigsaw-pieced the story

of a neighbor who stuffed her children—we never
knew how many—into one bed the way we forced
crayons of varying length and degree of damage

into a battered Crayola box. She threw more kindling
in the cast-iron stove, sat and waited for her man.
His shotgun lay on the kitchen table. Or stood

in a corner, or rested on the floor beside her chair.
Our missing puzzle piece: what was his Saturday night
misdeed? Were we older, we might have conjectured

an illicit tryst, carousing in a smoke-filled back room,
gambling away the egg money she hoarded for little
winter coats. He burst through the door either

reeling or slouching, boisterous or morbid, penitent or
arrogant. Accusations were exchanged. Or maybe not.
The truth was known by only one woman and one man.

But he lay on a blood-red swatch of kitchen floor
as she crossed the pasture to our uncle's place. Politely
asked that Homer drive to town and notify the sheriff.

We shuddered to think of all those fledglings safely
nested as their father bled on the floor. If he lived,
he would soon be out of hospital to give his woman

the beating of her life, our uncle guessed. His death
was ruled an open and shut case of self-defense.

White Girl Envy

The Chickasaw twins reigned on playground
and basketball court. Their arsenal included

hook shot, fast break, layup, intimidation
reinforced with magical twin telepathy.

Their waist-length twin braids whipped and
flipped like black lariats. So we had our mothers

French braid our strands into shoulder-length
squiggles, turnip beige or tree-bark brown.

Entering their teens, Rosetta and Juanita
visited a stylist who severed four iconic ropes,

which according to the sisters their mother
wrapped in tissue paper and tucked away

as relic. The family lived near Indian church
and brush arbor but the twins didn't go

to Sunday school. They spoke neither
Jesus admonition nor Holy-Roller hallelujah.

The basketball queens slighted our obsessions:
Elvis and rock 45s, teen fads and movie mags.

If a twin pierced us with disdainful glance,
we wilted like October sunflowers with

heads flopped. Oklahoma white girls ached
to be an *Ihoo himitta'*—a Chickasaw twin.

Back Row Religion

Town kids lined up in the last row
of church like ivories on a keyboard,
birds on a highline. My sister and I
raised the stakes by two when we
achieved our teens, left our parents
up front, gravitated to the cool kid pew.
Townies possessed all knowledge—from
Mantle's batting average to who had
an ace up the sleeve for the math quiz.
They sauntered through their little
world with ease and confidence.
Cheerleaders and athletes and stars,
they gave piano recitals, marched
in the school band, suited up
for competitive sports. Beneath the
watchful eyes of Jesus (or worse still,
Widow Baumgart) they passed notes
during prayer, tittered as the preacher
sermonized. We were thrilled and
terrified to be seated among them—
taking our chances, cutting the deck,
calling fate's bluff.

Firehouse

A fireman's daughter sneaked us past the man on duty
absorbed in some distraction at his street-level post.
The firehouse second floor—off limits to little girls—
smelled of tobacco, leather, grease, metal. A scary realm
outfitted with implements never seen in the mundane
world. Reminders that fire kills and firemen are big
and brutal. Because of the skeleton, also a haunted realm.
In the dust-mote haze of that upper-floor cavern,
a human bone frame slumbered in a plank box, the kind
where settlers deposited their dead in cowboy movies
we saw at The Holt on Saturday afternoons. Scary too
because that skeleton had once lived among us. Because
under ruffles and ribbons and curls, I am only this?
A cut-out floor circle positioned the firehouse pole.
One after another with intake of breath, we sprang
into airless void, wrapped the shaft with thighs and
elbows, ankles and fists. Glided down like firemen
into a mundane world where danger smolders.

II.

River Road

Rivers are the old roads, as are songs, to traverse memory.

-Joy Harjo, *An American Sunrise*

Removal

Uprooted from forest and bayou, farms and sacred spaces,
Thousands from the *Chahta okla* forded the Big Black,
Mississippi, Arkansas and Kiamichi to alien territory
Promised them so long as grass grows and rivers flow.

Her Wedding Night

Dressed in fine batiste for her deflowering,
Susan Moncrief McClain studied the stranger
on whose whims her life now depended.

James McClain was in Mulberry Grove a fellow
of up-and-coming promise—railroad surveyor,
student of law—studied by all of Sumter County.

Surveying local options, he chose the daughter of
a Choctaw planter rich in farmland and likely
to accept a cultivated white man's offer.

Fair skin luminous in lamplight, the surveyor
shed his garments, lifted the bridal quilt, sealed
the bargain struck with Susan Moncrief's father.

Confinement

Trapped in the four-poster marriage bed,
Susan finds no English word and none
in Choctaw to name the pain that claws
upward into her heaving belly, unmooring
womb and life. Cruel penalty for nights
her beloved entered there, murmuring
eternal fealty. Nine new moons the little
prisoner bided his sentence, battened on
jailhouse diet, waited to escape cradled
incarceration. Astride her spasms he
rides for freedom, now bravely crowns,
kicks, whoops his exit. A midwife healer
wipes, strokes, swaddles the tiny escapee.
In the canopy bed, Susan reaches to enfold
her firstborn, murmuring, "*Vlla nakni ossi,*
forever you belong to me."

Homestead

Susan heard stories of their agony in mud
and snow, of cholera and dysentery, those
of the *Chahta okla* who forded westering rivers.
But she was a moneyed Alabama woman,
mother of babies plump as ripening rosebuds,
married to a respected white lawyer, allotted
acres of pristine soil on Pearl River.

Susan dreamed the McClain farm would
evolve into a plantation beneath magnolias
with plate-sized blossom—its crops plentiful,
slaves dutiful. Starving Choctaws harried west
might well prosper in the Territory while
the McClains' mixed-race progeny inherited
a gem of an estate on the Pearl.

Governed

Born on a plantation in Alabama,
Susan McClain was twice removed
to Indian Territory. First the white-man
government bribed Choctaws to cede
their land to harvest-hungry whites and
become a transplanted Western tribe.
On the Poteau River with slave labor
to break soil and raise house and quarters,
the McClains presided over virgin acres
once ruled by scrub brush and cocklebur.

When homesick Susan pined for her mother,
the pioneers retreated to Mulberry Grove.
But government mandate forced them to
re-enact their Trail of Tears to the Poteau.
Aboard the steamboat *Alvarado*, captain and
crew extorted their cash. At Swallow Rock,
they buried two children dead of cholera.
Enrolled and quarantined at Fort Coffee
by governmental decree, they were issued
a year's rations and one government cow
to compensate their inconvenience.

Poteau Twilight

Chirruping cicadas
—like scratchings
of snare drums—
set evening's tempo.
In the cottonwood
grove a slight wind
shivers papery leaves.
A nicker from the
filly's stall and the
lowing of cattle
at intervals measure
the bars of twilight.
From slave quarters
a harmonica moans,
lullabies are crooned,
choral cacophonies rise
and fall in murmurs.
Inside the ranch house
a fretful baby rustles
the bedding that folds
her into the cradle.
Beyond the bois d'arc
the haunting howl of
a coyote proclaims
that Indian Territory
is not entirely
human property.

Bereaved

The remains of James Monroe McClain
lie in a pine coffin in the best parlor of
the Poteau River ranch house. Here again
arrives *illi,* Death, the uninvited guest
who stables his ebony-black mount in your
barn, plants hobnail boots under your table,
tousles the noggins of your little ones,
stretches full length beneath the quilt
beside you in the marriage bed.

Already, Susan, you have met him. Skirting
New Orleans to elude the plague, your family
boarded a steamboat to outrun the adversary.
Doe-eyed Helen and your unnamed newborn
he wrenched from their mother's arms. Then
Death strolled into Mulberry Grove, led away
your mother. He ambushed your father, who
vanished somewhere in Indian Territory, likely
murdered for the gold he carried.

Having stolen parents and progeny, Death
now pulls off the ultimate heist. Bereft Susan—
widow, matriarch, manager—you must bring up
seven fatherless children, decline the embrace of
an insistent bedmate in the four-poster beside you
in your husband's accustomed place.

Hearsay

Francis Marion Monks, another
Alabama man, favored well-heeled
Widow McClain, despite rumor
that her heart lay decaying in
Leard Cemetery up near Pocola.
Often we noticed Monks' saddle horse
hobbled in the Poteau ranch corral.
Sunday afternoons we watched
them take the air in a buggy behind
her pair of high-stepping roans.
We should've seen it coming—
the widow's second wedding.
Yet we wondered at the suitor's haste,
the woman's age, whether she was
again in the mothering way, if it
was not now for her too late. Had
the interloper courted with an eye
to adoption by the tribe? We
marveled at her vow to honor
and obey young Monks as
farming partner, companion to
her sons, housemate and bedmate,
iki of babies yet to come.

Her Death Song

Thou shalt no more be termed Forsaken; neither shall thy land any more be termed Desolate. . . for the Lord delighteth in thee, and thy land shall be married.

-Isaiah 62:4

With children and slaves and youthful strength, we
traveled a river road from easeful home to empty land,
yakni ikatoksalo. But earth is not owned, just rented;
payment exacted in blighted grain and blistered palms,
troubled nights, crops overripe, death out-of-season.
Until we learn we are earth's possession.

Husband, I sorrow that I bore you only one girl child,
failed to give you *vlla vhleha* to seed descendants
for this land of promise. Raise up my sons and daughters.
Lay me down beside my former love under the shaggy
post oaks in the *hatak aholopi* at Pocola. Souls ascend,
bones sleep for eternity beneath the Territory.

NOTES

Susan Moncrief McClain Monks (1819-1860) was an
Alabama Choctaw who, because of her race and her
family's ownership of plantation land coveted by white
settlers, was sentenced to follow a Trail of Tears to
Indian Territory (now eastern Oklahoma). She endured
displacement and homesickness; she grieved for children
who died on the trail; she founded a new home in a raw
country. Susan was my great-great grandmother.

Trail of Tears:

This term refers to the route to Indian Territory taken by the Choctaw, Cherokee, Seminole, Chickasaw, and Creek nations. U. S. Poet Laureate Joy Harjo (Muscogee/Creek) insists, however, that because there were many ousted Southern tribes, also many trails of tears.

Rivers:

The Pearl River flows from Mississippi and into Louisiana. Shortly after their marriage in 1834, James and Susan McClain settled on Susan's Choctaw allotment on the Pearl.

The Poteau River, tributary of the Arkansas, is located in southeastern Oklahoma. The McClains filed for land there in 1839 and—together with their slaves*— established a farm and ranch operation. They returned to Alabama, however, and remained for nine years. In 1849 they were forced to relocate permanently to Indian Territory, thus the return to their Poteau River property. James McClain died there in 1855.

In her death song, Susan McClain Monks recalls that she and her family traveled a "river road." The McClains' trail west was a water passage, not an overland trek (which could have proven even more horrendous). Their route followed the Tombigbee, Mississippi and Arkansas, as well as Lake Pontchartrain.

*Some members of the Choctaw tribe "owned" Black slaves. In these poems, the practice is not condoned, merely admitted.

III.

Wither Sooner than Desire

Ah, but a man's reach should exceed his grasp
Or what's a heaven for?

-Robert Browning, "Andrea del Sarto"

Visionaries

Addled and quixotic they seemed,
those stargazers who stocked rations
for man and camel—gold baubles and
perfumed balm too it was rumored—
and ambled off somewhere west. Their
destination, not one of them could tell.
Probably they would just meander,
schlemiels following a phantasm.
They had sighted a new star, some say,
or journeyed to anoint a future king.
Their testimony being foggy and evasive,
we were skeptical. We figured they would
become frazzled and weary, succumb to
hardships of the road or to the greed
of bandits. If you must be suckers, we
counseled, why not be marks for wealth
or women or notoriety—like other men?
What is the world to do with fools of faith?

Empress of Fair Eden, Snake Called Me

And sovereign Lady, Goddess among
gods. Sleek and enameled, his textured
body shimmered more than burnished
gold, coiled and uncoiled with grace.
His voice vibrated throughout my being
like melody of angel harps. He served
me fruit bursting with flavor—exotic
as nectar and ambrosia.

My human lover braided daisy stems
into a diadem for my brow. But flower
petals wither sooner than desire. He
addresses me not as goddess but
Woman to signify I am his. In the garden
beautiful Adam smelled of rose musk
and honey. Now he returns to our hovel
drenched in man sweat and the scent
of animal manure—hair and beard tangled
with twigs and burrs. We lie on piles of
dried grass and rushes. In lovely Eden we
nodded in a leaf-shade bower of asphodel,
pansies, hyacinth, violets—their blended
incense a celestial breath.

Manmaker Comes no More at Twilight

Maybe He doesn't know where I am.
Is sorry he evicted me over a forbidden
fruit snack and the fig-leaf apron my woman
made to cover my balls. I bet He misses shooting
the breeze with His smartest creation. Which
does not deny that Eve of the tangled curls
outshines every Eden flower. Whittled from
my rib bone, she acted like a queen, even
wanted to be smarter than me. But she took
no interest in Manmaker's rhetoric; instead
debated a two-bit slithering shyster who
stuffed her pretty head with bullshit flattery.

On my hardscrabble acres I met Chaos and
Hunger, predator and pest. I'm sentenced to
plow, plant and harvest; to nettles, weeds
and drought. A comedown to live by sweat
of my brow. Old Man Night now wraps Earth
in a black shroud. We'll retreat to my shack and
if Eve's migraine has faded, obey the command
to make a child. But my helpmate proves less
feisty and flirty outside Eden; our screwing
rehearsed, contrived. Besides, I don't want
a kid, being hardly more than a boy myself.
And lacking a reliable model of fatherhood.

Deception

Orpheus of Thrace—composer, musician, dazzling star—
ascends from gloomy Underworld into radiance of Earth light.
His lyre and voice stalled dog-hearted Cerberus, captivated
Hades, halted time, froze the Furies' writhing-serpent locks.
Orphean dirge restored to the singer his bride, reversed
     Death's cold certitude.

Orpheus whispers lyrics of passion, sings of the bower Eurydice
had decked with orange blossoms, listens for her weightless
tread, worries that she hesitates at Lethe's edge, has stooped
to tie her sandal and lost sight of him at a turning of the way.
Panic hints at godly fraudulence. Night chill shivers his frame,
     freezing expected mirth.

Causalities of Empire

In boiling smoke and ravenous flames that lap up the towers
and crunch the foundations of Ilium, Aeñeas tries three times
to clasp elusive Creusa. Three times she dissolves like mist

in morning sun, proving—as if proof were needed—
that she is an apparition, prophetic sign, mockery of
mortal desire. There's always something to incinerate love:

an aged father determined to burn with Troy, a small boy
to be led to safety, a god's mandate to thrive as founder
of Rome. Creusa must perish so that Aeneas may prosper.

Besides, the boudoir of Queen Dido awaits in Carthage,
a set design for theatrical coupling and suicidal parting.
Afterward, Aeneas will prove victor at Latium, become

object of the smoldering gaze of yet another princess.
Is he guilt-ridden by the immolation of Trojan Creusa?
By flashbacks of Phoenician Dido's funeral pyre?

On Tour

New Orleans, Little Rock, Tulsa, Houston

The Dolly wagon rolls down the interstate
past bayou and woodland, granite hills and
oil pumpers. Backwoods Barbie takes to
the road in a two-million-dollar tour bus
loaded with wigs and bling. It costs a lot
of money, she says, to look this cheap.

Lubbock, Phoenix, Las Cruces, Las Vegas

Dolly has travelled a mighty distance:
Locust Ridge to red-carpet runway, mountain
cabin to glitzy mansion, Pentecostal girlhood
to secular sainthood. Smoky Mountain
wildflowers bloom wherever planted but
Dolly prefers to blossom coast-to-coast.

Bakersfield, San Diego, Sacramento, Fresno

Like a fat caterpillar navigating a flower stem,
the bus crawls alongside vineyard and orchard.
Highway is the ribbon that ties songstress to fans,
past to present. As a snail carries its house on
little shoulders, diminutive Dolly totes her
trunkload of old melodies and older memories.

Norfolk, Raleigh, Charlottesville, Tampa

From the window of her rolling real estate
Dolly spies magnolia blooms and the feathered
flames of mimosa. Almost tastes fried catfish, grits
and gumbo. A mountain daughter comes home,
as trashy-looking a tart as she aspired to be.
I never left it, she says. Nothing's ever gone.

Desire

Mennonite women controvert the Gaze,
Shun makeup, jewelry, slacks and fashion shoes,
Flatten unshorn locks beneath plain black snoods.
Wear homemade dresses that evoke bygone days:
Below the knee with high neck and full-length sleeve,
Made of fabrics that neither sparkle, shine nor cling.
Do they lust for spike-heel boots and skinny jeans?
Long to shake out their tresses to flutter in the breeze?
Linger in aisles of sexy underwear and frothy negligées?
Run hungry fingers along verboten satin seams?

Vacancy

In December a construction dumpster squats on the
driveway of the A-frame house on Swensson Street,
heaped high with mangled lamps, mismatched chairs,
a gray-striped mattress—detritus of a hidden life.
As years revolved, nothing changed at the A-frame.
No holly wreath, no stars and stripes adorned its façade;
the white slash of its off-kilter curtain moved to neither
left nor right. On the crippled deck no barbecue grill
appeared in summer and vanished when russet leaves
drifted beneath the maple. Did the late owner despair
over passion or loneliness or insatiable disease that gnawed
away tomorrow? Did he float beyond dreams and desires
and tree-dappled shadows on Swensson Street?

Weep with Hecuba

The setting.
Aegean waves fondle fore and aft a thousand ships
weighty with plundered gold and household gods,
breastplates and shields, blades and lances. Lurid
flames lick bombed-out towers of a besieged city.

ENTER the Greek Soldiers.
Entitlement sits upon them like a well-tailored mantle.
Empire, more desirable than gold, compels the battalion.
Hands and faces splotched with blood, they herd captive
women, plant land mines, explode a birthing hospital.

ENTER the Trojan Women.
Flooding tears etch scars on their smoke-stained faces.
Eyes reddened, skin chapped, hair shorn in sorrow.
Torn garments soiled with enemy semen drag through dirt
of a violated motherland. Bosoms throb for dead babies.

EXIT the Women, guarded by Soldiers.

ENTER Hecuba.
Why have you come to this shore, old grieving mother?
Your pleas will not spare civilians, nor your fury stoke
the justice you seek. No sons remain to repel the invader

and rebuild the city. No daughters survive to wail about rape and genocide, torched homes and slaughtered babushkas, a flattened theater with children hiding inside. Nobody left to weep with Hecuba.

Ascent

A seated brass Buddha—titanic, serene,
enlightened, well-draped and well-fed—
presides at morning meditation. Autumn's
muted sunlight filters through windowpanes,
casting leaf shadows that tremble across
a Persian carpet bracketed by prayer rugs.
Boosted upon zafu cushions, kneeling
congregants with heads bowed, eyes closed
follow a female voice that intones: "Inhale
and feel the act of your breathing; exhale
and experience your breath as life."
Outside, a gospel band prophesies that
on some glad morning we shall arise.
Somewhere a motorcycle accelerates
(fly whine, mosquito buzz, cicada choir).
The leader's voice invites, "Receive the
moment as it rises up to meet you."
Praise singers respond, "When I die,
Hallelujah by and by, I'll fly away."

IV.

This Swirling Largesse

To Nature's voice attends from month to month,
And day to day, through the revolving year.

-James Thomson, *The Seasons*

Spring with Coronavirus

The lead Iditarod musher with 14 sled dogs
halted for breakfast today in Ruby, Alaska.
That's big sports news since the NBA called
time out, NASCAR stalled, March Madness
yielded to sanity. Stadium and cafe, pubs
and shopping malls stand all but deserted.
Churches stream Sunday service performed
before empty pews. At the vacant city park,
freezing rain glistens on quietly greening
fescue and drooping heads of crocus.

In social-distance quarantine, I recall an old
movie in which the remnant of humankind,
nuclear smitten, expires Down Under. In the
final scene a bedraggled banner reading
"There's still time, Brother" drifts ironically
above a deserted Melbourne street. Children
of Cold War phobia, we imagined our demise
by H-bomb fallout, not by silent pathogen.
Is this the way the world ends? Is this the way
we end with neither bang nor whimper?

April's in Town Again

I hear rumors that she
 arrived early this year. They say
  she will either stick around awhile
   or cruise on down the highway
    to check out her options.

I've sought a glimpse of her
 turning a corner,
  loitering in the park,
   hanging out at the playground
    where kids practice soccer.

I listen for her
 familiar titter beneath the new moon,
  piercing laughter at Ől Stuga bar and grill,
   mischievous giggle stifled by breeze
    on Coronado Heights.

I'm told that she
 flashes her azure eyes at all the locals,
  flounces a pink-and-yellow skirt,
   sashays around town, leaving behind
    a fragrance redolent of blossom.

I assume that she
    doesn't give a green goddamn, that flirty tart who
      teases our sensations,
        rekindles our hope,
          breaks our hearts.

Cicada Corpse

Clearing debris from last year's garden,
I uncover the crust of a cicada. Excepting
one missing leg, it is intact. Almost whole,
despite late winter's ferocity. I place
the insect shell in my palm, noting
its wide brow built for headlamp eyes
like those on a vintage Jeep. A black
crenelated border trims the head.
Celestial wings—enviable by angels—
are labyrinthine veined, translucent
as isinglass. The creature lingered
seventeen years below ground to
assume this intricate, decorated
body that housed scant weeks of life.
How very extravagant of Nature.

Resurrection

On Easter Sunday myriads of paper butterflies
strung on fishing line swarm the sanctuary
from balcony to chancel. Pastor Amy
climbed a 30-foot ladder to loop strand
upon strand of the hand-colored beauties
around the pinnacle of a polished wooden
cross that hangs above the altar. Resurrected
from the church's crypt of seasonal décor
and commissioned as squadrons of symbol,
the fragile insects flutter on air currents,
cast shadows that brindle the empty cross.

Encounter

With the entitlement of leviathan, a behemoth
blade for a wind turbine surges past. I glance out
the window of my compact to observe its gargantuan
   passing   passing   passing
as it swims up the river of highway that is I-35.
In the Midwest we often sight them, strapped
on oversized truck and trailer like a sperm whale
lashed to Ahab's *Pequod*, tapered fluke dipping
to the rhythm of semi wheels slapping pavement.
They travel in pods of three, the shimmering
whiteness of their backs and bellies stark against
atmospheric waves of Kansas-blue sky.

Tornado Alert

The good-looking Channel 12 weatherman has stripped off
his jacket, loosed his tie to assure me that he remains
vigilant, hard at work protecting me through the
night. He points out Kansas hotspots where
storms percolate, funnels form. I recall nights
of weather-sponsored terror in Tornado Alley. We
children were toted from house to storm cellar
where we huddled trembling next to rows of
Mason jars filled with Mother's labor—fruit,
beans, jellies--all for naught had we been
scooped out of the earth by Oklahoma
twister. In the Omaha cyclone I rushed
children and poodle to the bowels of our
house as tornadic winds smashed 4,000
buildings, flung cars around I-80.
I live alone. Even our tabby cat
died last winter (the one that
despite feline protest we
contained belowground
during tornado watch).
I am old, tired, unafraid.
Flicking the remote, I
zap the handsome
weatherman into
a mist of pixels,
give myself up
to a greater
power than
any mortal
vigilance.

Boneyard

Pickup bed stacked high with tree trimmings,
leaves and twigs stripped and scattered
by hailstorm, branches downed in Kansas wind,
I pull up to the boneyard brush pile and empty
my load of organic castoff. This smoldering
Gehenna perpetually consumes our town's
remains from storms, disease and pruning;
has done so longer than most of us can
remember. Chore completed, I guide the
decrepit Chevy truck back home to heap it
again with sycamore rib, mulberry clavicle,
walnut vertebrae. Nature's cycle (greening,
growth, catastrophe, blight, death) ends with
a flourish—in plumes of ascending mortality.

Sideswipe

Twenty-four hours post-op and solaced by oxycodone,
I glide homeward on I-35 with a friend behind the wheel
of my lipstick-red Chevrolet. The black SUV must have

shadowed us for a while, parallel on our left and traveling
at a 70-mph speed that matched our own. Without preamble
I'm yanked from nirvana by a single jolt and the shriek

of bludgeoned fiberglass and steel as chassis nudges chassis,
body bounces off body, door panel slashes front wing.
Both drivers pull right of the roadway, assess damage,

photograph respective auto wounds: black on red, red on black.
In a sedated haze, I watch from an air-cooled interior as
my companion, her auburn mane shimmering in July sun and

flailed by Kansas wind, wraps up formalities and slides back
in the driver's seat. She pours the injured Chevy into a cascade
of speeding traffic as I ponder which gash will bleed me more:

a black underscore sliced on my red polymer panel
or the scalpel swipe across my belly.

Futility

Killing the dove might have been easy if
killing is in one's DNA. The juvenile bird with
its one good wing fanned blades of grass;
the other wing hung mangled, bloody.
I considered suffocation in a plastic bag.
Or breaking its neck as Hardy's Tess did
for Wessex pheasants winged by hunters.
Then the grounded flyer looked at me.
I found I could not snuff out life even as
    kindness to the slain.

I brought sunflower seeds on a plastic lid,
water in a yogurt cup, eased my offering
into the columbine thicket where the bird
hovered on the brim of life. For two days
the dove signaled if not gratitude at least
awareness of my overture. Then it vanished,
leaving neither limp carcass nor clutch of
bloodied feathers. My patient no doubt
became a predator's morsel, the dove's
    death my personal failure.

Intercession

Your Autumn came calling this week,
a multi-hued harlequin to dance us
into December. Your gales shimmied
chrysanthemums, scattered leaves and twigs
more lavishly than petals strewn for a bride.
Racks of black walnuts plunk onto my lawn
like billiard balls discharged on a pool table—
a toothsome feast for squirrels.

Yet I plant tulip bulbs in dirt seven inches
down and dry as ash. Inside shrouds of
blowing topsoil, farmers sow winter wheat.
Cattle forage, wade knee-deep in shrinking ponds.
No rain in the forecast, no cloud in the firmament.
With this splendor of color, this swirling largesse
of design and dance and plenitude, would it seem
presumptuous to murmur a plea for rain?

Nostalgia

At some indefinable point prior to
        the sere and yellow leaf,
you acknowledge owning more behind
        than you anticipate before.
More adventures finished, fewer setbacks
        up ahead. The latter tending to
life or death prognoses, not to scaling peaks
        or besting torrid waves.
If you're lucky, that benevolent artist Memory
        paints you a sky impossibly blue;
puffed clouds innocuous as the beard of God;
        a childhood entirely of firecrackers
and tooth fairy, May baskets and birthday cake.

October Blue Moon

delicate ornament
dangled above
the treeline

ghostly balloon
levitating

colossal pearl
aglimmer

aery nothing
inspiring dreams

antique coin
coveted and pricey

silver discus
snuggled in
bare branches
of cottonwood

communion wafer
dissolving in
October dawn

wax circlet
pasted on the
sealed envelope
of summer

Winter Hike

From Canterbury to Whitstable
a trail wanders into forests mantled
in mist, beyond a fourteenth-century
church, its lichen-speckled gravestones—
longtime neighbors—leaning left and
right companionably. We pass a fallow
field, corduroy plowed, its wales dusted
with wintry fog. Then a picnic circle, racks
of firewood, hectares of shoulder-high
grasses that whisper, hum and tremble.
We arrive at darkness and the sea,
collapse on chalky dunes, listen to
the crash of waves in anapests that
measure our panting breaths.

Writer's Block

My Muse in winter behaves like a Grizzly sow—
constipated and cranky—hibernating in chthonic
caverns. Other times she's a burnished russet
vixen concealed within multi-hued foliage,
elusive as shaken quicksilver. Or a doe bounding
into a forest of metaphor, too agile for pursuit.

I meander, lost in a thicket, chasing a phantom
like Arthur's knights seeking in vain the Holy Grail.

I require instead a swan, elegant and stunning,
exquisitely reflected in aquamarine water. Or
a lissome cat, electric-furred and self-absorbed,
licking a particular itch into paroxysms of joy.

Wintering Over

The season's first snowfall powdered Kansas prairie
        today like flour sifted onto a rolling board.
Nearby meadows have been mowed clean, the
        landscape now a tabletop with hay-bale
muffins tossed randomly across the expanse.
        On an unmown meadow three horses
lower black velvet muzzles among strands and
        clumps of brittle bluestem and foxtail,
souvenirs of summer drought. Nine horses had
        boarded in that meadow this summer.
Sometimes you'd see them convened at a salt lick
        (chestnut, buckskin, pinto, a couple each
of bays and sorrels, one palomino, a blackie with
        white blaze). Or maybe they'd trot from
all directions to meet a pickup truck whose driver
        downloaded baskets of—I don't know—
yellow corn or worm-pierced apples deemed
        unfit for human palate. I wonder about
their six grazing companions absent from the
        meadow today. Perhaps they've been moved
to winter pasture. Or warm, nightdark stalls with
        guarantee of dry provender—mounds of hay
to last until the meadow thaws and grass-green blades
        shoulder their way through mud into light.

Referendum

We the aggrieved hereby notify you of intent to
   Turn you out. We have long suffered from
Your fickle reign, cold indifference to our plight.

You launched a first campaign in pristine garb—
   White as bridal veil or christening dress.
Disarming as dancing waves or tumbling cumulous.

At the outset, we adored you, couldn't get our fill
   Of carols and snowmen, glug and gaiety. Now
Your pranks—arbitrary and capricious—merely annoy.

Enough swirls in the driveway and spills on sidewalks.
   Enough frozen pipes, motors, fingertips.
More than ample our commutes on glazed rivers of ice.

Thus we shall oust you—stash snow shovel in garage,
   Tire-tread boots in nether region of closet.
Nurture spiteful thoughts of your dirty brown demise.

Surfeit

How many watercolor
sunsets are sufficient?
Does a human get her fill
of ocean chant, lilac scent,
seeds of dandelion skydiving
by silk parachute, robins
preening orange breasts?
I have counted blackbirds
perched on power lines like
children queued for recess.
Admired glistening chain
mail on rainbow trout.
Sauntered under leafy
canopies on pine-needle-
cushioned paths. Captured
snowflakes on my tongue,
insects in my hair. As remedy
for humdrum days, make
your house green.

Following an Oklahoma girlhood and a high school teaching career in Nebraska, **Linda M. Lewis** makes her home in Lindsborg, Kansas, where she settled in 1987 to become a professor of composition and British literature at Bethany College. Now retired, she indulges in family time, sleeping late, leisurely lunches, reading poetry, and poetry readings. As professor and literary scholar, she published four books and a number of critical essays on authors Dante and Dickens, Blake and Shelley, George Eliot and George Sand, John Milton and Elizabeth Barrett Browning—among others. She is the author of a poetry collection, *Ensemble* (Spartan Press, 2019), and has published here and there in various poetry magazines.